Suzie's Messy Room

Diane N. Quintana and Jonda S. Beattie

Copyright © 2022 Release Repurpose Reorganize LLC

All rights reserved. No part of this publication may be reproduced, distributed, or transmitted in any form or by any means, including photocopying, recording, or other electronic or mechanical methods, without the prior written permission of the publisher, except in the case of brief quotations embodied in critical reviews and certain other noncommercial uses permitted by copyright law. For permission requests, write to the publisher at the address below.

ISBN 978-1-7359684-4-5

Printed in the United States of America

ReleaseRepurpose.com

My name is Suzie.
I am five years old.

This is my family.
I have a mother, a father,
and an older brother, Joe.
Joe is eight years old.

This is my room.

I have lots of fun
playing in my room.

Sometimes, I have so much fun playing in my room that all my toys, dolls, puzzles, and stuffed animals get mixed up together.

Then my mother says, "Pick up your room."

What do I do when my mother asks me to pick up my room?

I sit in the middle of my bed and cry because I am so little and the mess in my room is so big!

But what do I do when my mother asks me to pick up my clothes?

I play the "seek and sort" game.
I find all my dirty clothes and
put them in the laundry basket.

Then I find all my dress-up
clothes and put them in
the dress-up basket.

I put my clean clothes away
on the shelves in my closet.

What do I do when my mother asks me to pick up my books?

I find my books
from all over my room.
Some are under my bed.
Some are on my bed.

I put the books from all over
my room in my bookcase.

What do I do when my mother asks me to put my dolls and the doll clothes away?

I pick up my dolls and put them in the chair and on the toy shelf.

I line up their shoes on the next toy shelf, and I put their clothes in the doll's trunk.

What do I do when my mother asks me to pick up my puzzles?

I find my puzzle boards and match up their pieces. Then I put them on my toy shelf.

What do I do when my mother asks me to pick up my stuffed animals?

I put my three favorite stuffed animals on my bed. Then I toss the rest into the animal hammock in the corner of my room.

I laugh because it is too full. Some of my animals fall out of the hammock and land back on the floor!

What do I do when my mother asks, "I think you may have too many stuffed animals now. Why don't you pick out ten to give to some other children to love?"

I give a big sigh.
That makes me sad.
I love ALL my stuffed animals.
Which ones am I going
to give away?

I ask my mother, "If I choose eight of the larger stuffed animals, would that be okay?"

My mother smiles and says, "Yes!"

I get one of my mother's laundry baskets and put a soft towel at the bottom to make a little bed.
Then I choose eight of my stuffed animals, give them a kiss goodbye, and lay them in the basket to go to their new home.

My mother says that some other boy or girl will love them just as much as I do!

Now my other stuffed animals have room in their hammock.

What do I do when my mother says, "You have done such a wonderful job in your room! Where would you like to go for a treat?"

I laugh and say, "Let's go to the ice cream shop where they put sprinkles, whipped cream, and cherries on top of my ice cream!"

NOTE TO PARENTS

This book was written for parents and children to share.

The authors took some basic organizational strategies:
- Break projects down into small manageable steps
- Sort like with like
- Cull collections
- Assign a place or a home for belongings
- Reward for jobs completed

The authors then applied these strategies to the common task of picking up a room.

People are often overwhelmed when given what to them seems like a large project. The first step is to break the project down into small manageable steps.

Study the illustrations. Notice that Suzie did not do a perfect job. You will see that there are some doll clothes not perfectly put away and that the bookcase is a bit untidy. Still, Suzie did a great job for her age and her efforts are accepted and praised.

We encourage parents to accept the organizing job done by their child so as not to minimize the child's efforts.

There is also a reward for completing the task. As professional organizers, the authors encourage their clients to reward themselves when a project is complete. Rewarding Suzie shows appreciation for her effort.

OTHER BOOKS FOR CHILDREN BY DIANE AND JONDA

Benji's Messy Room by Diane N. Quintana and Jonda S. Beattie

Benji is a typical, active five-year-old little boy. He loves playing with all his toys in his room and sometimes creates a real mess! When his mother asks him to pick up his room, Benji is overwhelmed and doesn't know how to begin. Benji's mother helps him complete the job by breaking the project into small tasks that Benji is able to finish easily. Doing this teaches Benji how to get organized.

Basic principles of organizing included in this story:
- Break projects down into small steps
- Sort like with like
- Cull collections
- All belongings need a home
- Reward for completed tasks

OTHER BOOKS BY DIANE AND JONDA

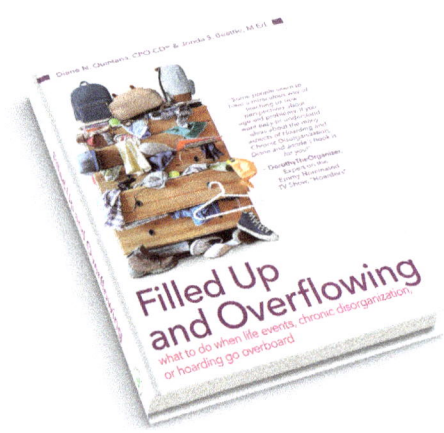

Filled Up & Overflowing was written to help you and your family members, friends, and spouses find answers to questions and concerns about the safety and comfort of their loved one in their space.

ABOUT THE AUTHORS

Diane N. Quintana is a Certified Professional Organizer® through the National Association of Productivity and Organizing Professionals (NAPO) and a Certified Professional Organizer in Chronic Disorganization® through the Institute for Challenging Disorganization (ICD®). She is also a presenter and best-selling author.

Diane N. Quintana is a former elementary school teacher. She is the owner of DNQ Solutions, LLC a professional organizing company in Metro-Atlanta that works with both residential and small business clients.

Jonda S. Beattie is a professional organizer, presenter, and best-selling author.

Jonda S. Beattie is a former elementary special education teacher and a former lead teacher of special education with a master's degree in special education. She is the owner of Time Space Organization a professional organizing company in Metro-Atlanta that works with both residential and small business clients.

Both Diane and Jonda are active members of NAPO, NAPO-Georgia, and ICD®.

In 2020, Diane and Jonda founded Release Repurpose Reorganize, LLC. Their vision for working together is: To empower you to cultivate better health, better relationships, and a better lifestyle.

Our mission is to guide you to build your refuge in the world. To release, repurpose and reorganize what you own so it serves you instead of you serving it.

ORGANIZE YOUR HOME 10 MINUTES AT A TIME DECK OF CARDS

Parents: use this deck of cards to help you organize your home in short 10-minute segments of time.

These positive cards will motivate you to declutter, organize and simplify your stuff.

Each of the colorful 50 cards outlines 4 – 6 simple steps to organize and accomplish 1 task in a 10-minute time span.

An added benefit is that you can involve your children as some of the cards are labeled Child-Friendly.

All you do is pick a card from the deck, follow the step-by-step instructions, and you are done in 10 minutes or less.

Easy peasy!

This deck of cards is made in the USA and available to purchase at:
www.releaserepurpose.com/organizingtools

HOME SOLUTIONS COURSE

The Home Solutions Course begins with The Basics. This course is for the person who would like to do it on their own but wants some guidance.

The Basics module sets the stage and gives you basic information you can apply to almost every area of your home.

If you want more detailed information, instruction, and ideas for organizing specific areas within your home check out the following modules:

Organize Your Bedroom

Organize the Bathroom

Organize the Closet

Organize the Kitchen and pantry

Organize the Home Office and Paperwork

Organize the Laundry

Organize the Family Room/Dining Table

Organize the Children's Room

Organize the Garage, Carport, Shed House

This course (**The Basics**) and the modules listed above are available for purchase on our website:

https://releaserepurpose.com/organizingtools

www.ingramcontent.com/pod-product-compliance
Lightning Source LLC
Chambersburg PA
CBHW051319110526
44590CB00031B/4410